MAGNETIC FLYERS

Instant Fill-in-the-Blank Brochures that Are Sure to Attract People to Your Events

by Norm Daniels

LIGHT FORCE

Basic Instructions and Tips

By following these step-by-step instructions you can create eye-popping, attention-getting brochures, flyers and posters to promote your youth program. Each section of this book contains specific instructions to guide you.

1. Choose a brochure, flyer or poster and remove it from this book (the pages are perforated).

2. On scratch paper write out any information that you will add to the brochure, flyer or poster.

3. Using a typewriter, computer, rub-on type (available from a graphic arts store—follow the manufacturers' directions), clip art from Section 6 at the back of this book or a pen, letter your specific information on the original flyer. Make sure that your text will fit in the space provided on the page. (You might want to create a rough draft on a copy before making your final version—this way you can check your spelling and can estimate how much room you need for the information you are adding.)

4. Check your masterpiece and clean up any shadows and blemishes that might print.

5. Find a photocopy machine and print the number of copies you need. Many copy machines can be used with a variety of colors and types of paper. Be creative. Optional—use highlighter pens to add a little color to your copies (highlighters will not smear the copy toner).

6. File the original. Then send out, hand out or post your finished copies.

7. Take the rest of the day off!

Additional clip art can be added to the art in this book. **The Youth Worker's Clip Art Book, The Youth Worker's Son of Clip Art Book!** and **The Youth Worker's I Was a Teenage Clip Art Book** are great resources for clip art, headlines and borders geared specifically toward youth (all of these are available from Gospel Light Publications or your local Christian supplier).

Section I...

Two-Sided, Three-Fold Brochures

These brochures are virtually ready to send. Simply follow the steps outlined in the "Basic Instructions and Tips" on page 4 for adding information you need to promote your activities. (You may want to include a parent release section on many of these brochures.) Then follow the steps below for photocopying and folding.

Fold them like this:

1. Use a photocopy machine that will copy back-to-back (duplex). Or photocopy one side of a brochure, then feed the copies through the machine a second time to copy on the back (you will need to experiment to find out how to load the paper in the copier and which direction to turn your brochure master in order to get everything to line up). Hint: We have laid out the pages in this section so that the top of each page is placed along the perforation.

2. After you have copied both sides of a brochure, "letter fold" each one as shown in the sketch. Optional—use highlighters to add color to the copies.

3. Send them out and watch your program sell out!

CAMP

INFO

Load & Depart:

Return:

Cost:

STUFF TO BRING

Who to Contact

STUFF to DO

Glam Up Today!

Registration Form

Name: _____ Age: _____

Address: _____

Phone: _____

Summer Camp

SIGN UP TODAY

INFO

SPONSORED BY:

SUMMER CAMP

The Official... Registration Form

Name: _____ Age: _____

Address: _____

Phone: _____

CHECK THIS OUT!

This is gonna be Hot!

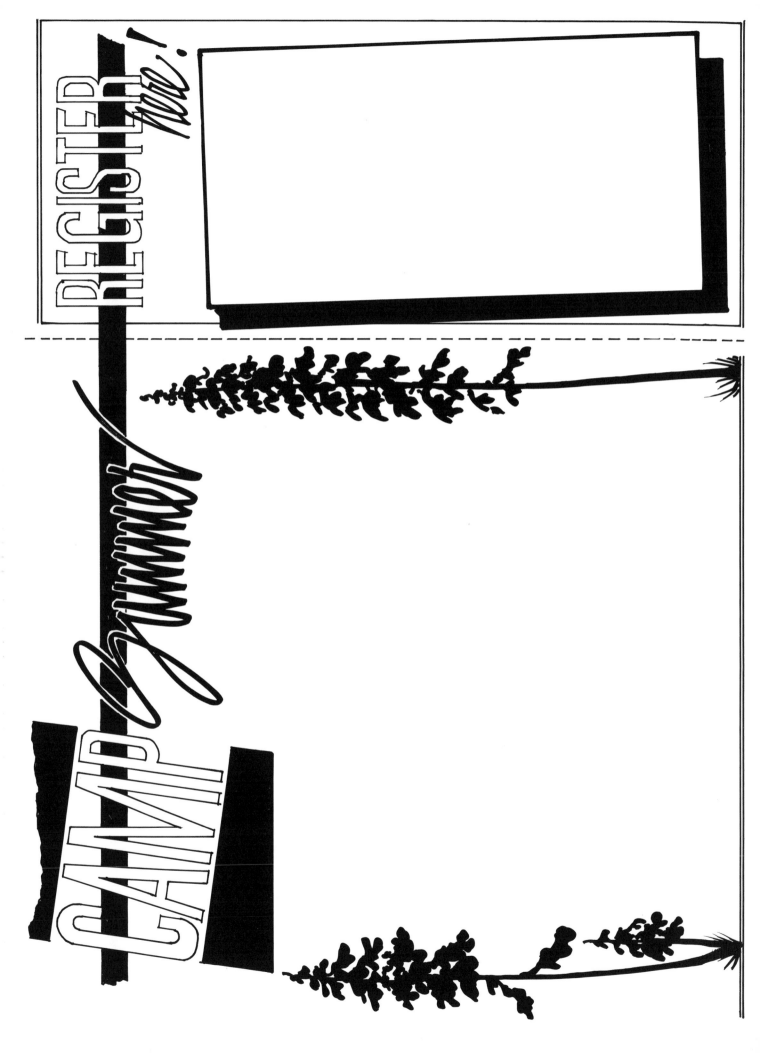

REGISTER Now!

CAMP Brummon

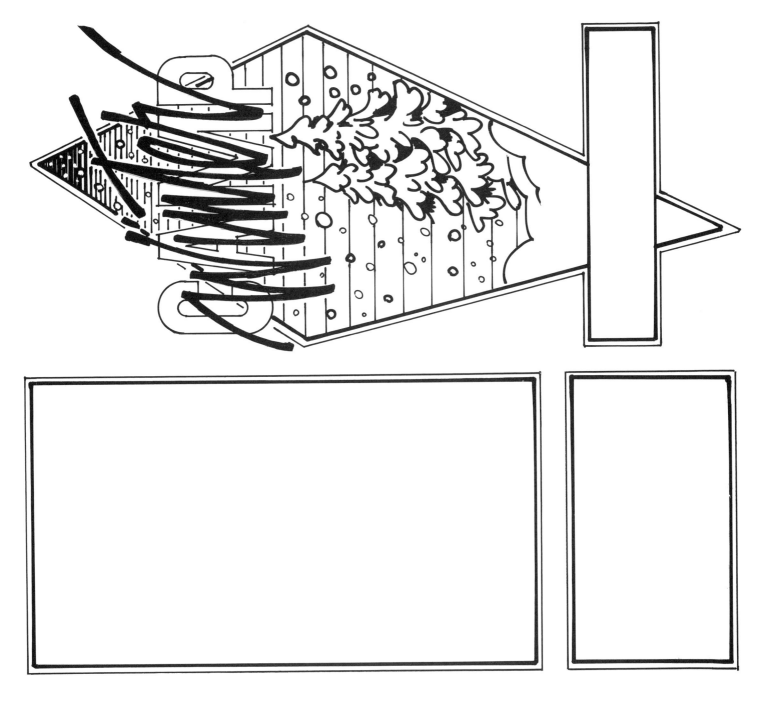

WINTER FUN!

Winter Camp Registration

Name: _____

Age: _____

Address: _____

Phone: _____

Winter Camp

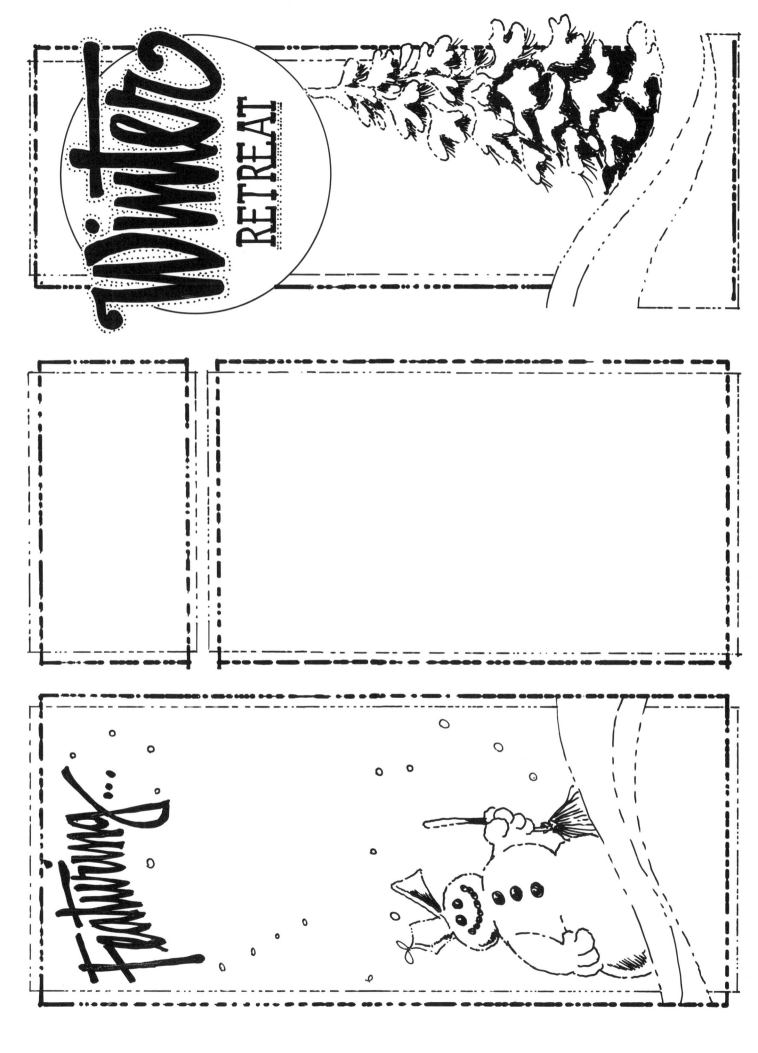

Winter Camp
RETREAT

Featuring...

Registration for Winter Retreat

Name: _____ Age: _____

Address: _____ Phone: _____

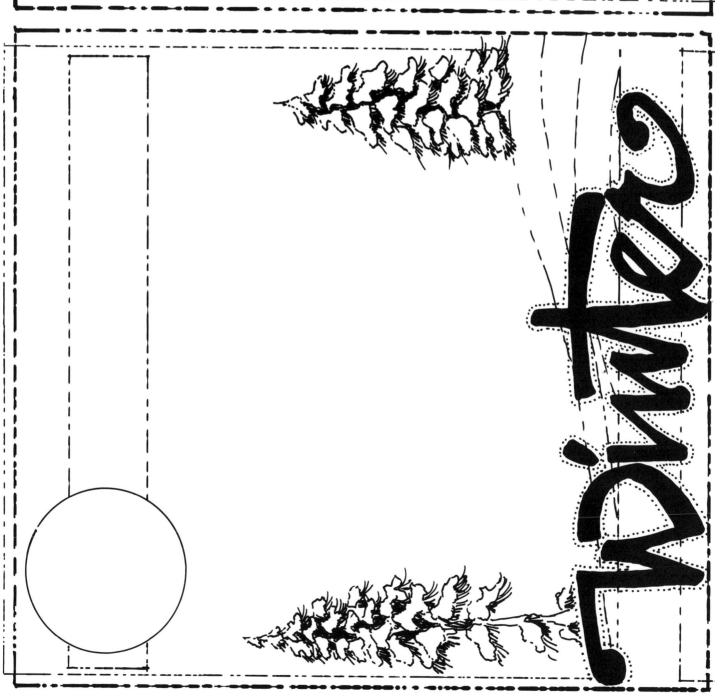

WEEKEND

RETREAT

GENERAL INFO

SPONSORED BY

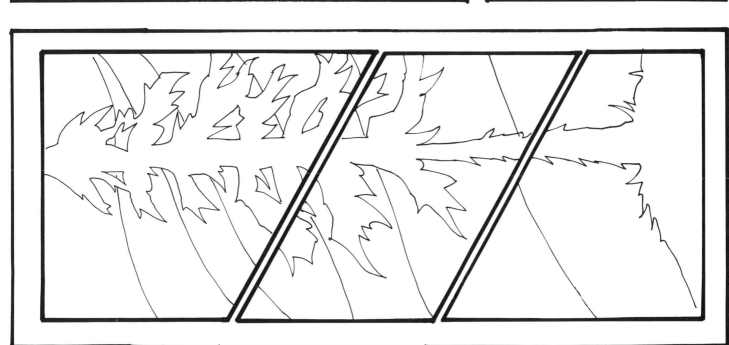

REGISTRATION *for the* BIG RETREAT

NAME: _____

ADDRESS: _____

PHONE: _____ AGE: _____

THE BIG RETREAT IS HERE!

TIRED OF THE 'OL SAME 'OL THING

Upcoming Events...

. Map .

SCREW MORE

JOIN US EVERY WEEK

FOR SOMETHING NEW & EXCITING!

CHECK THIS OUT

WHAT? (glad you asked)

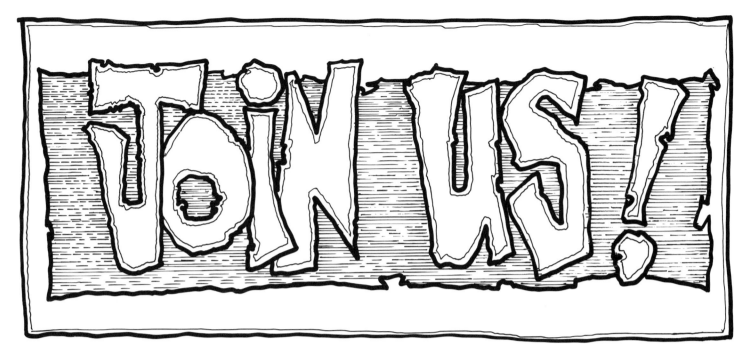

MAP... TO WHERE WE ARE
(WHERE YOU WANNA BE)

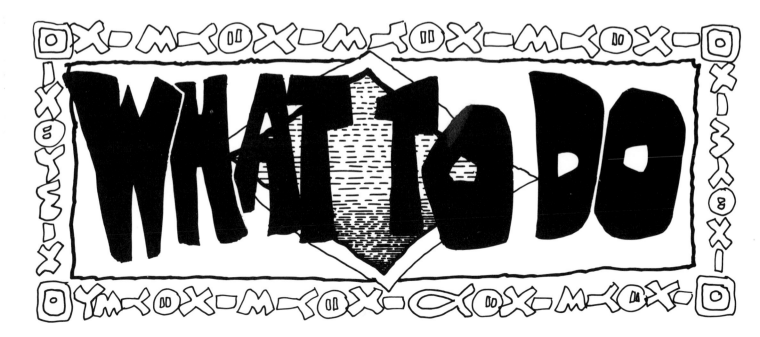

FRY·A·THON

WHAT To BRING

- sunburn protection — SPF 1000 TAN
- God's Holy Word — HOLY BIBLE
- sleeping bag
- recreational equipment
- sunglasses
- overnight stuff: toothbrush, towel, smell control, undies, etc...
- feet protectors
- anti-mosquito spray — BUG OFF
- swim suit

TO·DO

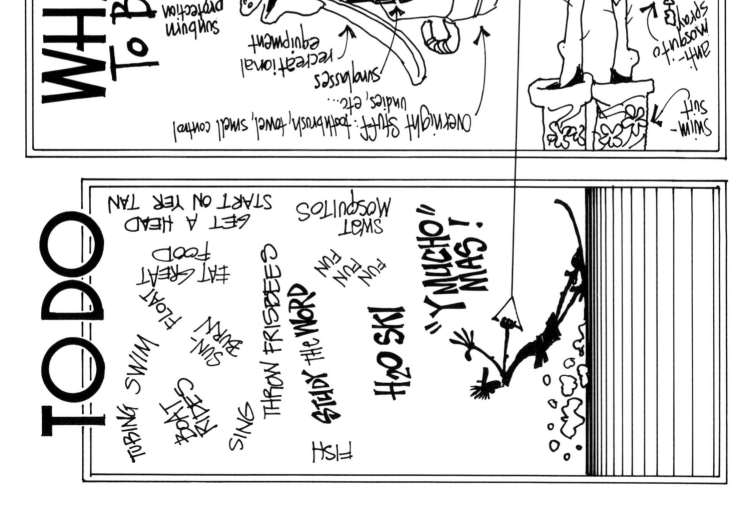

- TUBING
- SWIM
- SUN-BURN
- FLOAT
- CLEAN CREEK
- SING
- THROW FRISBEES
- EAT GREAT FOOD
- STUDY THE WORD
- SWAT MOSQUITOS
- FUN FUN FUN
- GET A HEAD START ON TER TAN
- H₂O SKI
- FISH
- "Y MUCHO MAS!"

FRY·A·THON REGISTRATION...

NAME:_____

ADDRESS:_____

PHONE:_____

FRY·A·THON

A T T H E   R I V E R

Sponsored By:

SPONSORED BY

THE RIVER

NAME: _____

ADDRESS: _____

PHONE: _____

FAVORITE KIND OF TREE: _____

PARENT RELEASE FORM (O BOY)

THE BEST RIVER TRIP EVER!

Section II...

ONE-SIDED, THREE-FOLD BROCHURES

These brochures are similar to those in Section 1, except they only have print on one side and they are folded a little differently. Again, follow the steps outlined in the "Basic Instructions and Tips" on page 4 for adding information you need to promote your activities. Then follow the steps below for photocopying and folding.

1. Find a photocopy machine and run off as many copies as you need (pretty simple, huh).

2. You may want to use highlighter pens to add a little color to the copies. Then "Z fold" each copy as shown in the sketch.

3. Now they're ready to distribute.

4. Oh, yeah—when these are opened up they can also be used as small posters for your bulletin board or can be displayed around the church or a school campus (contact the school to find out their policy about posting promotional materials).

SPONSORED BY:

SKI TRIP

Reach OUT

Section III...
Half-Page Handouts

Here's a cheap way to produce lots of quick handouts.

Again, follow the steps outlined in the "Basic Instructions and Tips" on page 4 for adding the information you need to promote your activities. As you can see, there are two identical handouts for each activity, so you will need to prepare two sets of added information. Then follow the steps below for photocopying and cutting apart the copies.

1. It's math time! Figure out how many handouts you need. Then divide that number by two. This equals the number of photocopies you need to make (since each copy equals two handouts—are your math muscles getting too much of a workout?). Make your photocopies.

2. Cut the copies apart down the middle of the page as shown in the sketch (watch your fingers).

3. Distribute your handouts by tossing them en mass over your group, by neatly stacking them and then passing them down the rows of your obedient, well-behaved kids or by forcing them on unwilling individuals.

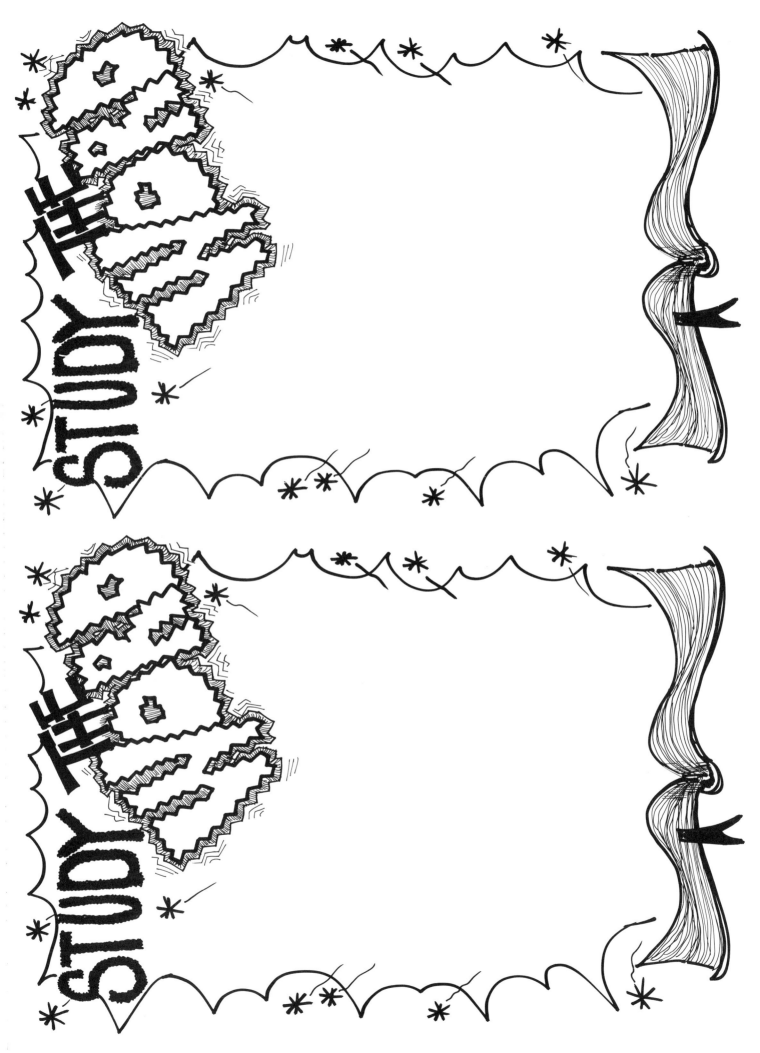

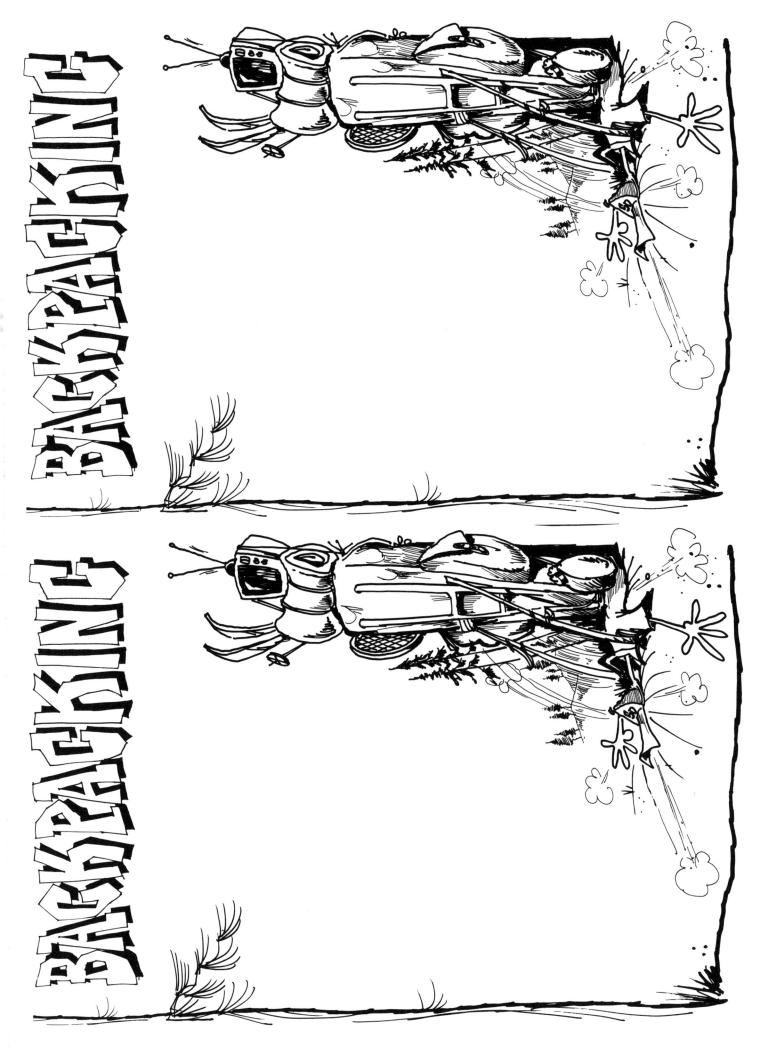

Christmas
BANQUET

Christmas
BANQUET

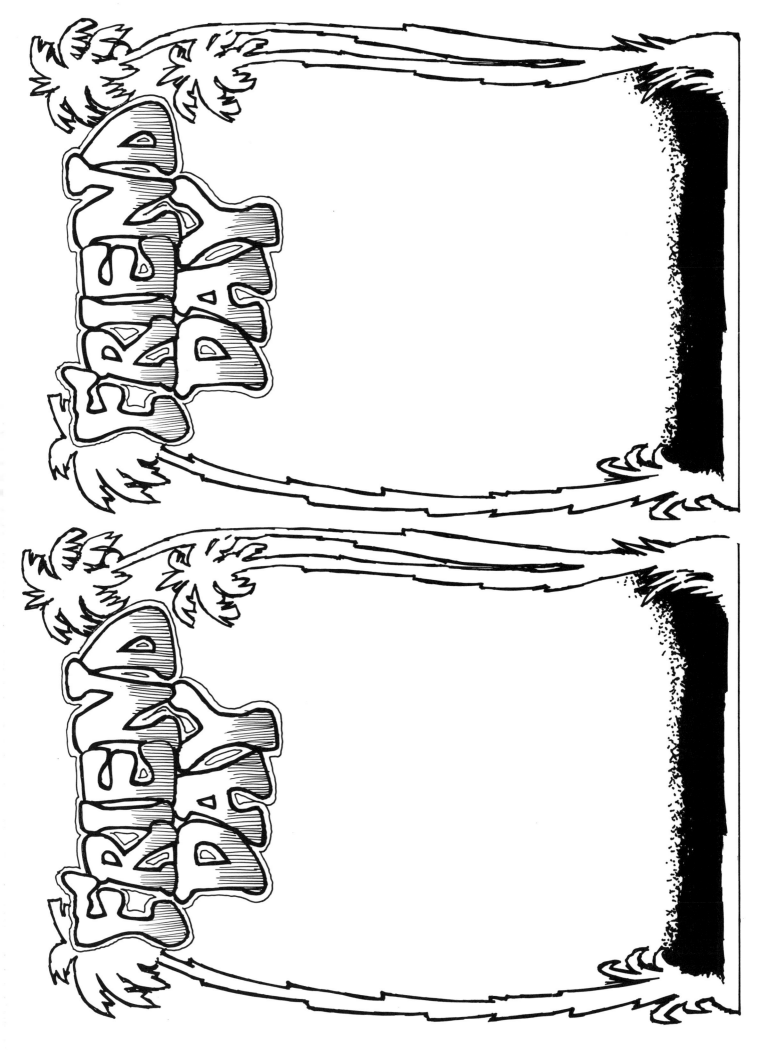

CRUISE
to
Catalina Island

WHAT TO DO: HIKE, GOLF, SWIM, SCUBA DIVE, FISH, BOAT RIDES, SKIN-DIVE, BIKE, SHOP, EAT, WINDSURF, JET SKI, PARA SAIL, or JUST RELAX!

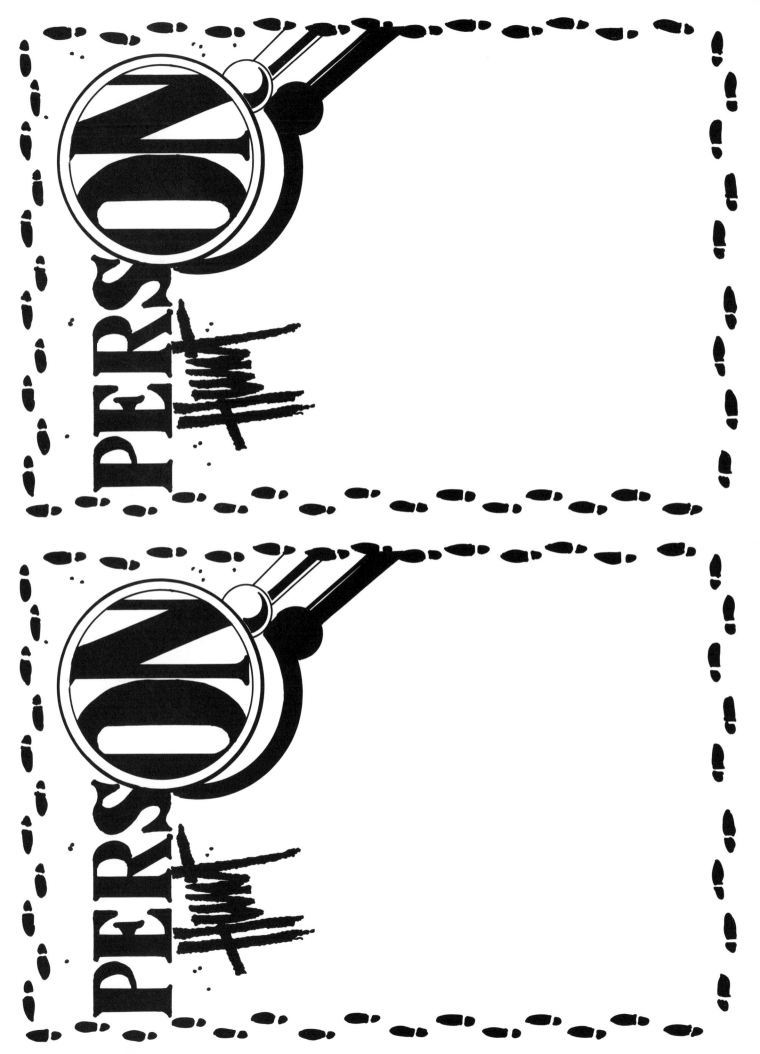

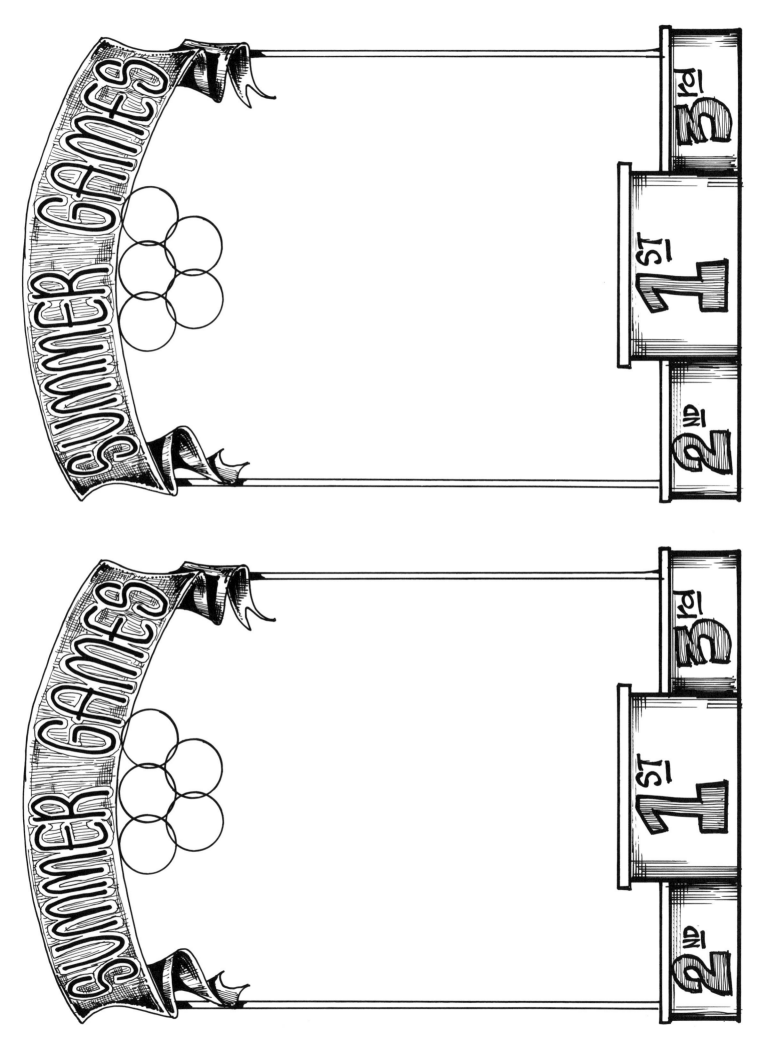

Designer SPUD Party

Decorate a potato
(and yourself to match).

Prizes will be awarded for the top **3** taters!

After the Competition: **A HOT POTATO FEAST!**

Featuring loads of gastronomical
wonders to top off your taters.
(Don't worry, we won't eat your designer spuds.)

Where:
When:
All This and More for Only $__!!

Designer SPUD Party

Decorate a potato
(and yourself to match).

Prizes will be awarded for the top **3** taters!

After the Competition: **A HOT POTATO FEAST!**

Featuring loads of gastronomical
wonders to top off your taters.
(Don't worry, we won't eat your designer spuds.)

Where:
When:
All This and More for Only $__!!

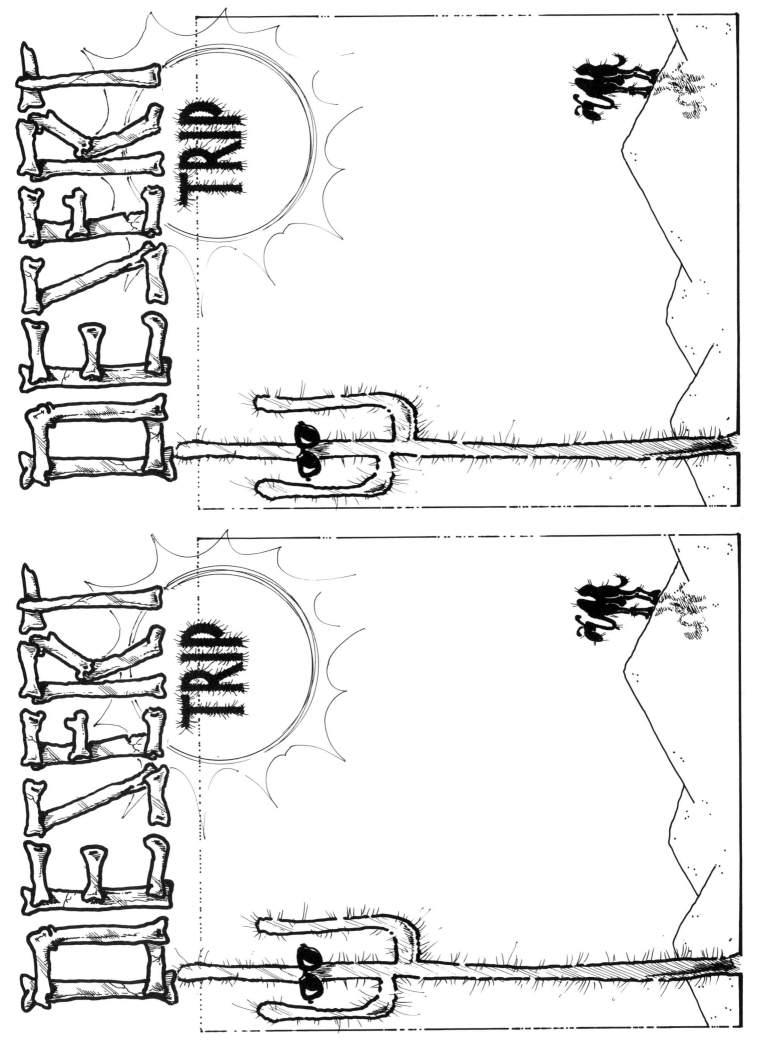

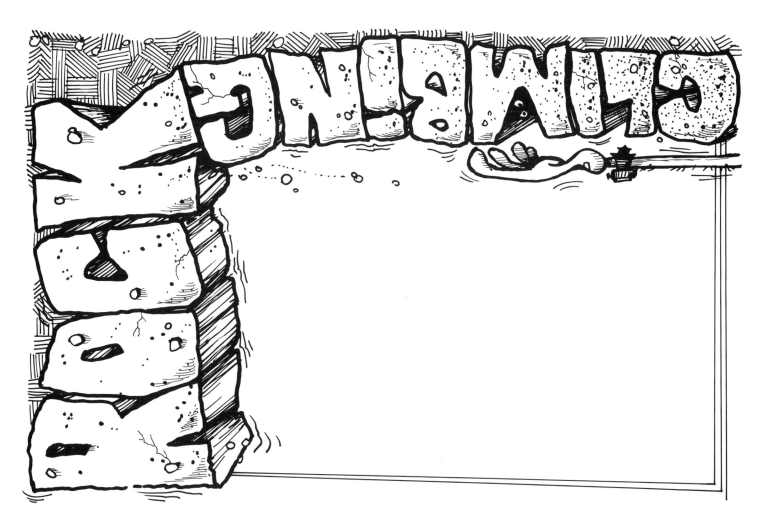

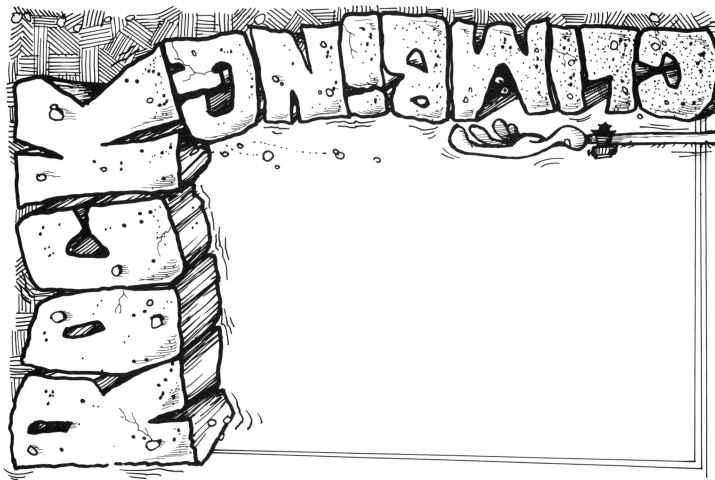

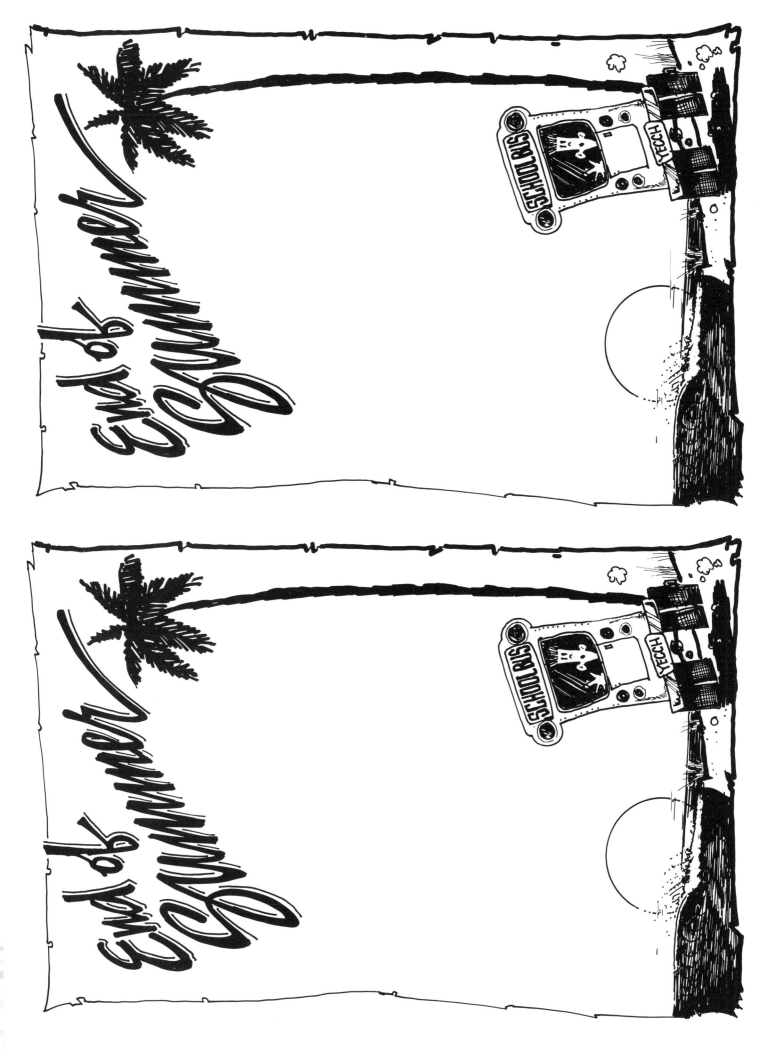

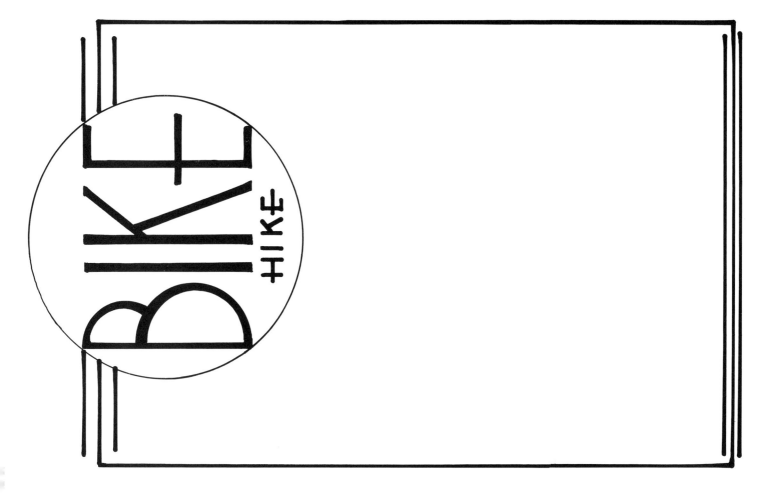

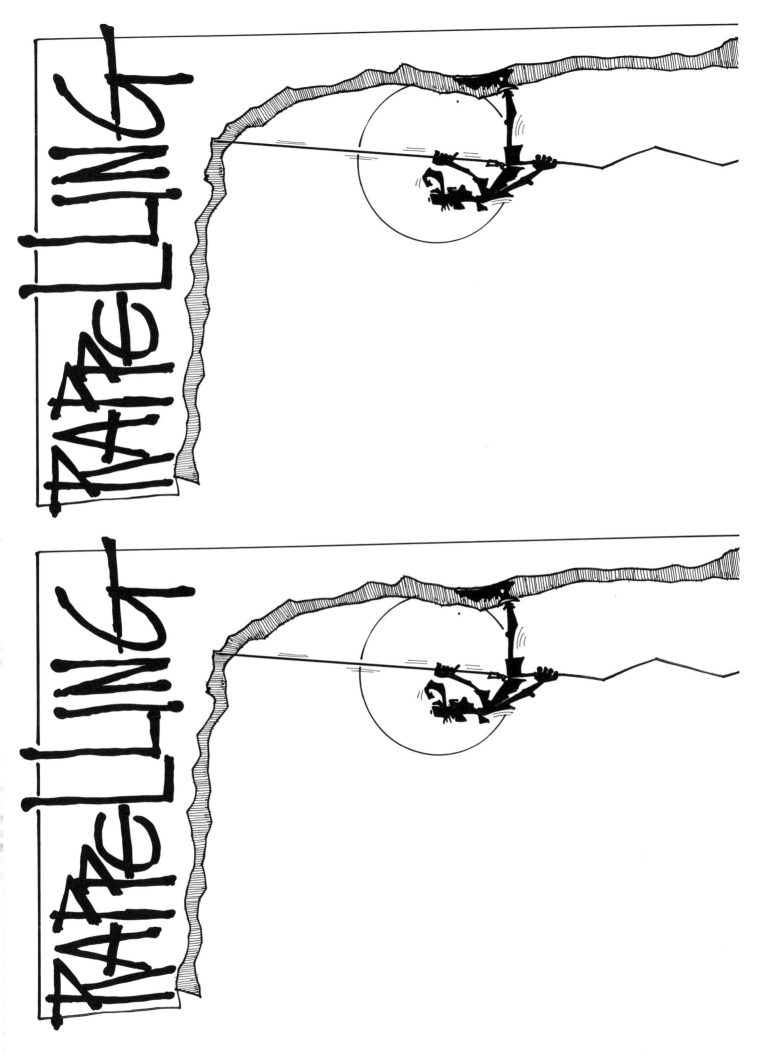

SECTION IV...
FULL-PAGE POSTERS

Use these pages to advertise your program by posting them around your church, the school campus (talk to those in charge at the school first) or across the planet.

Add any needed information (see p. 4 for instructions). It is a good idea to keep this information to a minimum so that the poster doesn't become cluttered-looking and communicates effectively. Then make a bunch of copies (using colored paper or card stock and highlighter pens will increase their appeal) and get out the tape or staple gun.

Be creative!

last grasp...

Summer Blowout

TONIGHT
After Church

ALOHA
BASH

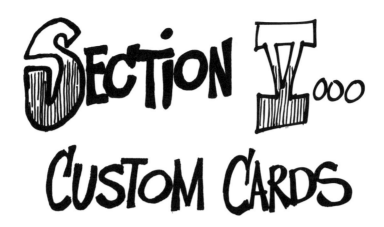

Section I ooo
Custom Cards

Use these cards to send notes of thanks or encouragement to those who support or participate in your youth program. Photocopy the cards, then fold them as shown in the sketch. Write brief notes on the cards, put them in envelopes and send them off. Doing this on a regular basis will build support for and interest in your program.

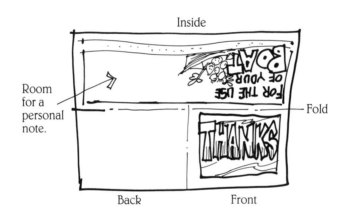

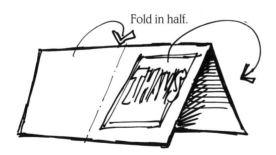

Now it's ready to go!

THANKS

For letting us use your BOAT

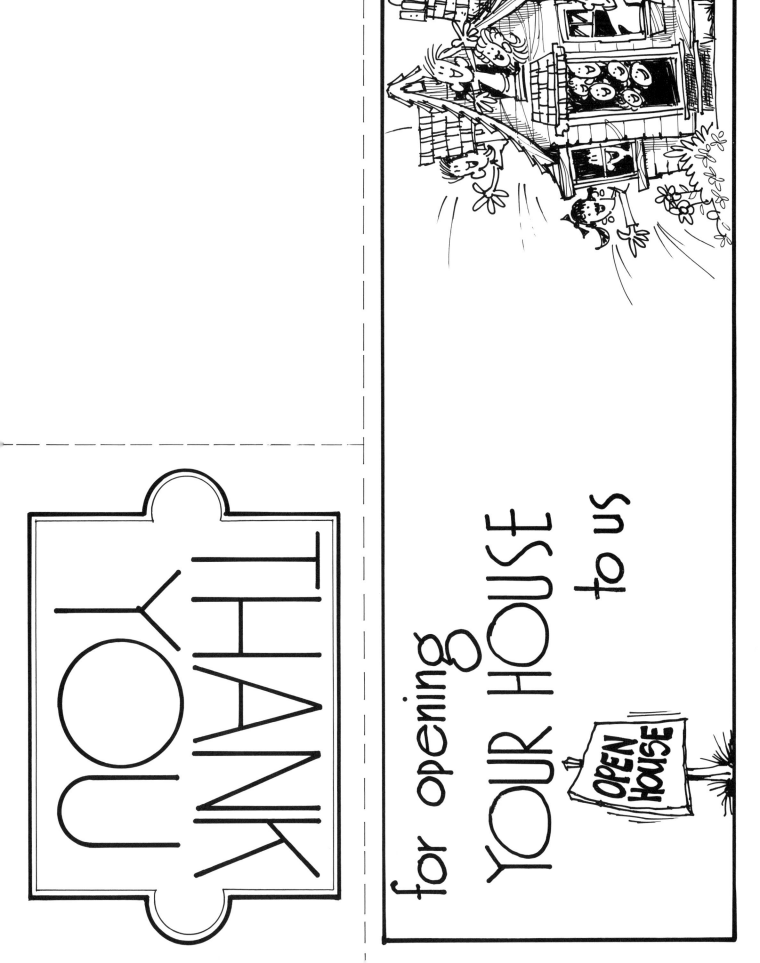

THANK YOU

for opening YOUR HOUSE to us

OPEN HOUSE

FOR DRIVING THE BUS

THANK YOU

FOR ALL YOUR HARD WORK

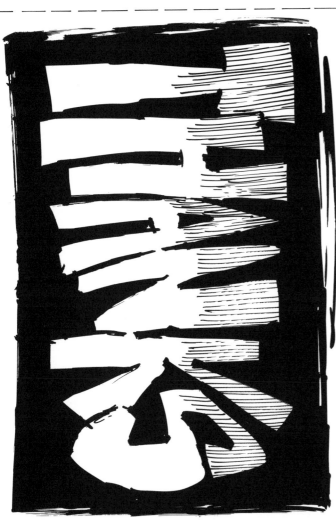

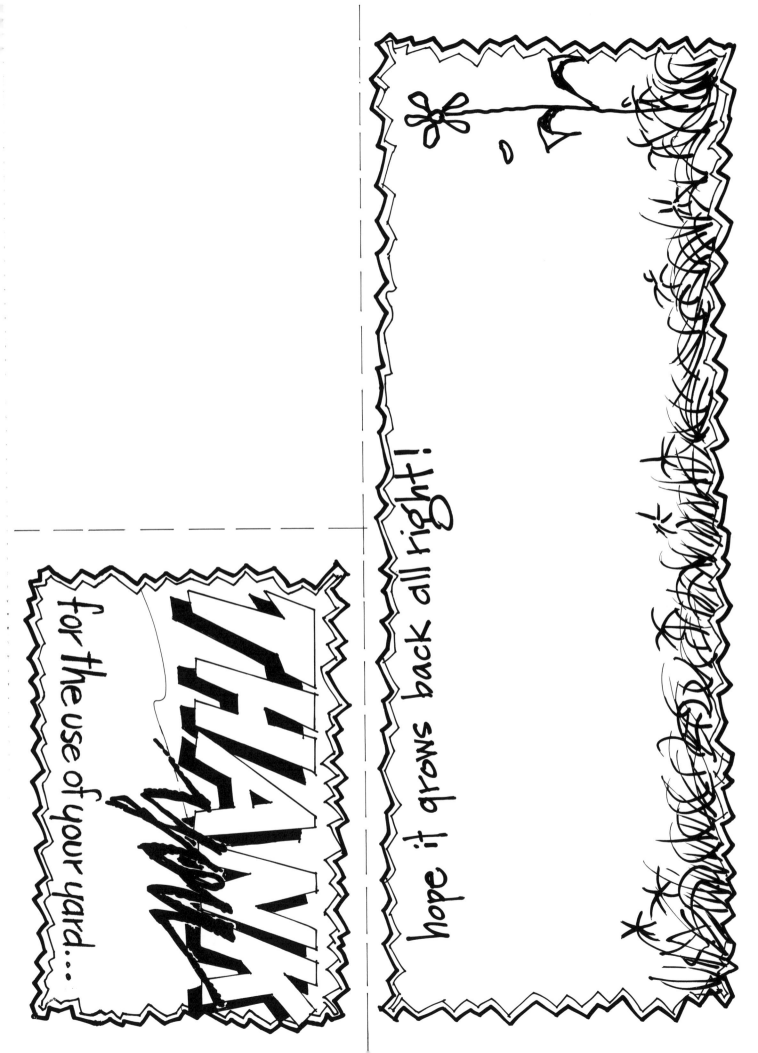

THANKS

for the use of your yard...

hope it grows back all right!

THANK YOU

FOR SPEAKING

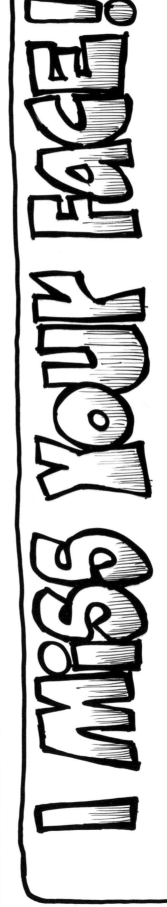

Use these dates, times and costs to add specific information to your brochures, flyers and posters. Just cut them out and glue them in place (glue sticks work great for this).

Fall Winter Spring Summer

Fall Winter Spring Summer

Fall Winter Spring Summer

Admission Price:	**Admission Price:**
Who:	**Who:**
What:	**What:**
When:	**When:**
Where:	**Where:**
Why:	**Why:**
How:	**How:**
How Much:	**How Much:**
Where to Meet:	**Where to Meet:**
Sponsored By:	**Sponsored By:**
Parent Release Form:	**Parent Release Form:**

January February March
April May June July August
September October
November December

1 2 3 4 5 6 7 8 9 10 11 12 13 14 15 16
17 18 19 20 21 22 23 24 25 26 27
28 29 30 31 $1.00 $2.00 $3.00 $4.00 $5.00 $6.00

$5 bucks $7.00 $8.00 $9.00 $10.00 $15.00 $20.00 $25.00

$10 bucks $30.00 $35.00 $40.00 $45.00 $50.00

JANUARY FEBRUARY MARCH APRIL
MAY JUNE JULY AUGUST SEPTEMBER
OCTOBER NOVEMBER DECEMBER

1 2 3 4 5 6 7 8 9 10 11 12 13 14 15 16 17
18 19 20 21 22 23 24 25 26 27 28
29 30 31 $5.00 $10.00 $20.00 $30.00 $40.00 $50.00

January February March
April May June July
August September October
November December ....

1 2 3 4 5 6 7 8 9 10 11
12 13 14 15 16 17 18 19 20
21 22 23 24 25 26 27 28 29 30
31 $1⁰⁰ $5⁰⁰ $10⁰⁰ $20⁰⁰ $25⁰⁰
$30⁰⁰ $35⁰⁰ $40⁰⁰ $45⁰⁰ $50⁰⁰

June July August
1 2 3 4 5 6 7 8 9 10 11 12 13
14 15 16 17 18 19 20 21 22
23 24 25 26 27 28 29 30
31

January February March
April May June July
August September October
November December
Spring Summer Winter Fall

1 2 3 4 5 6 7 8 9 10 11 12 13 14 15 16 17 18 19
20 21 22 23 24 25 26 27 28 29 30 31

JANUARY FEBRUARY MARCH APRIL

MAY JUNE JULY AUGUST

SEPTEMBER OCTOBER NOVEMBER

DECEMBER 1 2 3 4 5 6 7 8 9 10

A.M.

P.M.

WINTER

SPRING

SUMMER

FALL

GET INVOLVED DON'T MISS OUT WE NEED YOU!

PING GAMES Friends FUN Music

PIZZA SINGING Bible Study

Monday Tuesday Wednesday

Thursday Friday Saturday Sunday

Monday Tuesday Wednesday Thursday Friday Saturday Sunday

Monday   Monday Tuesday Wednesday Thursday Friday Saturday Sunday

Tuesday Wednesday Thursday Friday Saturday Sunday

MONDAY TUESDAY WEDNESDAY THURSDAY FRIDAY SATURDAY SUNDAY Monday

Tuesday Wednesday Thursday Friday Saturday Sunday

Monday Tuesday Wednesday Thursday Friday Saturday Sunday

Monday Tuesday Wednesday Thursday Friday Saturday Sunday

$1 $5 $10 $15 $20 $25 $30 $35 $40 $45 $50

$55 $60 $65 $70 $75 $80 $85 $90 $95 $100

Be There   Join Us!   Good Stuff
Don't Miss Out!   Hot Times
Bring a Bible   Bring a Friend
Bring a Snack   Special Speaker
Sign Up Today   Check This Out

$1 $5 $10 $15 $20 $25 $30 $35 $40
$45 $50 $60 $70 $80 $90 $100

Friends Fun Food Music Bible Study

Bring a Bible Bring a Friend Singing

We Need You! Pizza Mystery Guest

Special Speaker Featuring Prizes

Fall Winter Spring Summer

Sign Up Today Check This Out

Prizes   Games   Friends   Fun
Food   Music   Singing   Pizza
Special Speaker   Bring a Bible
Bring a Friend   Bible Study

Be There Join Us! Pizza
Good Stuff   Don't Miss Out!
Hot Times   Bring a Bible
Bring a Friend   Bible Study

Prizes   Games   Friends   Food
Music   Singing   Special Speaker
Bible Study Bring a Bible   Pizza
Bring a Friend   We Need You!

BE THERE   GOOD STUFF
JOIN US!   DON'T MISS OUT!
HOT TIMES   BRING A BIBLE
BRING A FRIEND   PIZZA

THE END

At last... my back hurts!

Special Thanks to...

- Patsy, Jessica and Joseph Beach Daniels (my wonderful family);

- My dad, who got me started drawing;

- Ralph, Scotty, Phil, Pat, Rich and Tim—these guys gave me some great ideas (and said they'd buy this book);

- Murf and Steve at SMBC—for using my brochures for years (now I'll get paid for them);

- And Bob Phillips at Hume Lake—for giving me a kick start.